The writer of this book is a secondary school student. He earned a scholarship at his school, the writer also has passions for electronics as he makes small functional devices that serve as a way of learning

Ahmad Faisal Alyousuf

SPACE AROUND US

AUSTIN MACAULEY PUBLISHERS®

LONDON * CAMBRIDGE * NEW YORK * SHARJAH

ISBN – 9789948732709 – (Paperback)
ISBN – 9789948732693 – (E-Book)

Application Number: MC-10-01-9097053
Age Classification: 6-9

The age group that matches the content of the books has been classified according to the age classification system issued by the UAE Media Council.

First Published 2024
AUSTIN MACAULEY PUBLISHERS FZE
Sharjah Publishing City
P.O. Box [519201]
Sharjah, UAE
www.austinmacauley.ae
+971 655 95 202

Table of Content

All Planets

Here are all the *eight* planets: Mercury, Venus, Earth, Mars, Jupiter, Saturn, Uranus, and Neptune. Four of these planets are known as the rocky planets because they consist mainly of rocks. Mercury, Venus, Earth, and Mars are rocky planets. Jupiter and Saturn are called gas giants. Gas giants primarily consist of gas and are massive. And then there are Neptune and Uranus, which we call ice giants because they are made of cold gases.

Sun

The sun is huge! It's so big that you could fit 1,000 Jupiters or 1.3 million Earths inside it. You are alive today because of the sun, which provides the world with heat and sunlight. It takes light about 8 minutes to travel all the way from the Sun to Earth. That's a long time! It means sunrise and sunset could happen 8 minutes sooner than we think.

Mercury

Known as it's the smallest planet in the solar system, Mercury is shrinking every second. In fact, Mercury is small enough to fit inside Europe. Yes, it's that tiny.

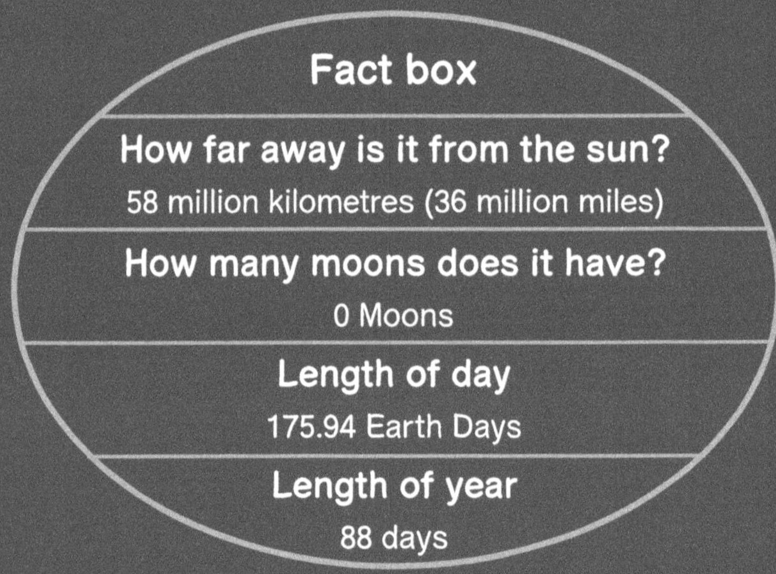

Venus

Venus is often called 'Earth's twin' because it has a similar size. Venus has a thick atmosphere; heat from the sun can come in, but it can't escape. That's why Venus gets extremely hot, with the temperature usually around 475 degrees Celsius (864 degrees Fahrenheit).

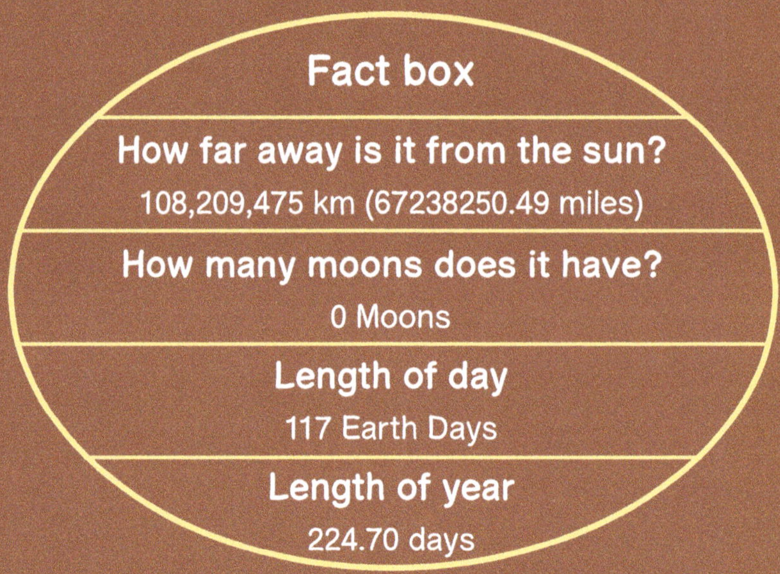

Earth

Earth is our home planet. You might think it's massive but compared to the gas planets, as I said, it's tiny. And did you know, most of our planet is covered in water? Only 30% of the Earth's surface is land. Every four years, we have a special leap year because our year is actually 365 days and 6 hours. That's why we add an extra day to February, making it 29 days instead of 28!

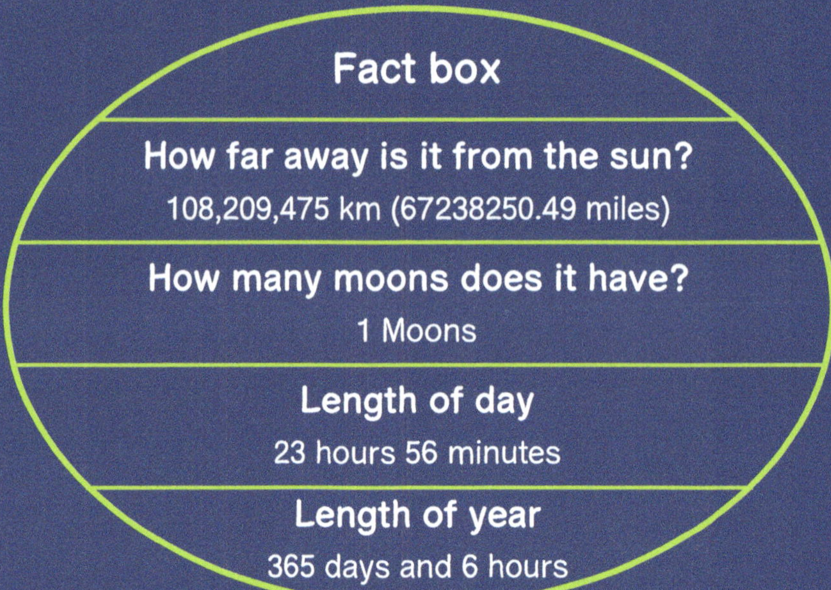

Mars

Mars is called the red planet because it looks red, and that's because of the red sand and materials on its surface. Scientist think there might have been life on Mars, and they also believe there could have been water there.

Mars has two moons, known as Phobos and Deimos. And guess what? The tallest mountain in our solar system isn't Mount Everest, it is on Mars! It's called 'Olympus Mons,' and it is about 24 kilometres (16 miles) high, three times taller than Mount Everest. Like Earth, Mars also has a North Pole, which is filled with snow.

Fact box

How far away is it from the sun?
287 million km (178333532 miles)

How many moons does it have?
2 Moons

Length of day
1 Earth Day and 37 Earth Minutes

Length of year
88 days

Jupiter

Jupiter is the largest planet in our solar system, and it's truly gigantic. You could stack up 1,300 Earths inside of it. Jupiter has a super thick atmosphere, about 13,000 miles (21,000 KM) thick, way thicker than Earth's atmosphere which is only 60 miles. There is a famous red spot on Jupiter, it is actually a storm. The winds there can blow faster than a speeding car! "Fact" the winds there can reach speeds of 432 km/h (268 Miles per hour).

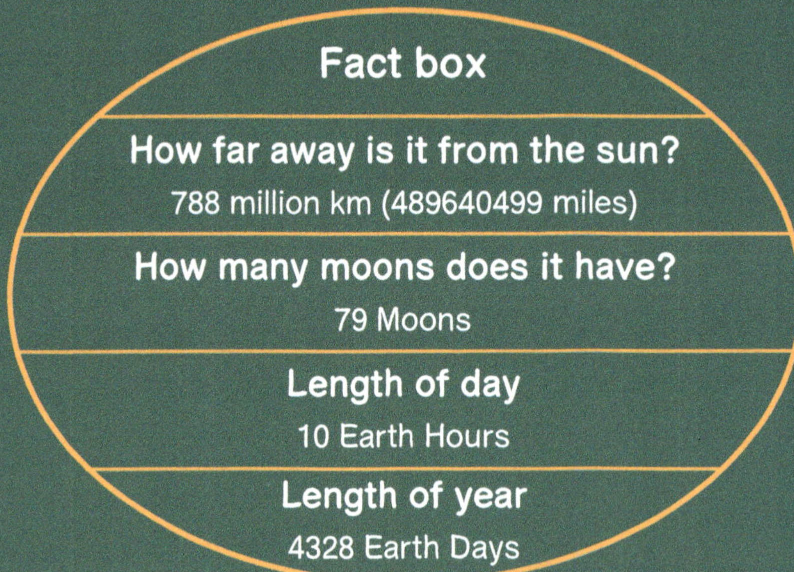

Saturn

Saturn is really special because of its beautiful rings, which are made of lots of rocks all stacked up together. And get this: while Jupiter has a bunch of moons, Saturn has more than 82 moons! Also, Saturn is a planet you can see from Earth without a telescope.

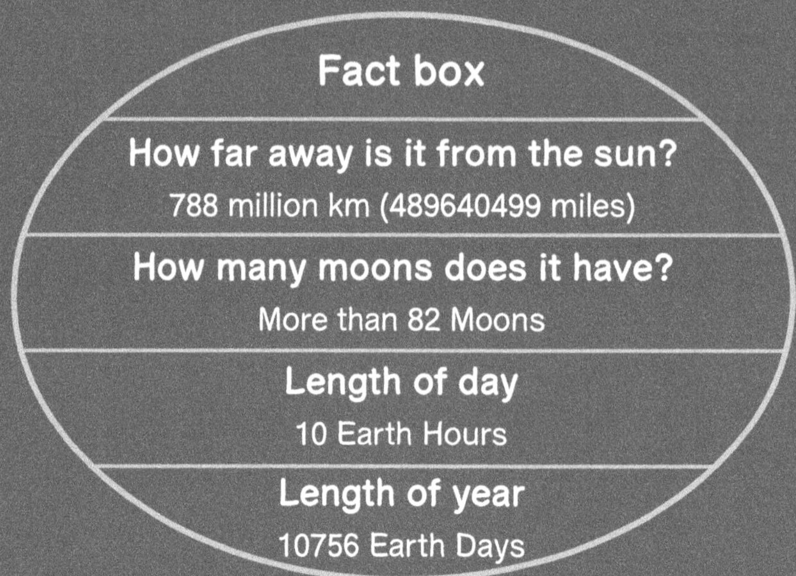

Uranus

Uranus is an ice giant, just like Neptune. It has 27 moons. Uranus spins on its side, which is pretty unusual! Uranus also has a thin ring around it, like Saturn, but much smaller.

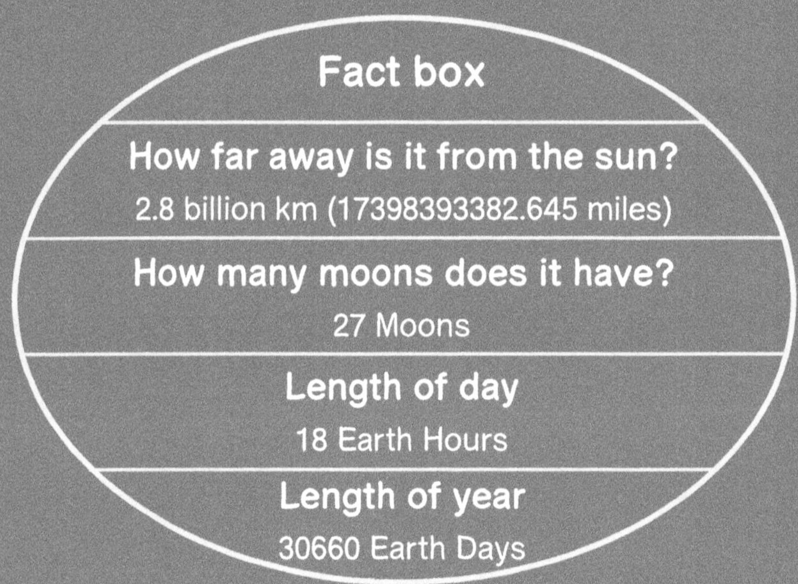

Neptune

Beyond Uranus is Neptune, the farthest planet from the sun. As a result, it is very cold, with temperature dropping as low as -128.889 degrees Celsius (-200 degrees Fahrenheit). Just to give you an idea, the coldest temperature ever recorded on Earth is warmer than that, at less than -73.3333 degrees Celsius (-100 degrees Fahrenheit!).

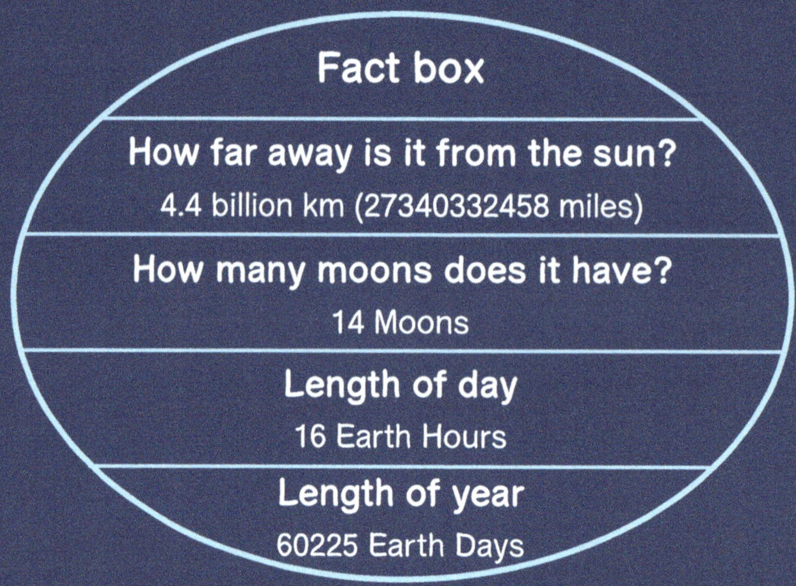

Fun Facts

All planets fun fact

- **Pluto**

Pluto is not a planet, but it's a dwarf planet.

- **Sun**

UY Scutti is the largest star, you could fit inside it more than 5 billion Suns.

- **Mercury**

A piece of Mercury was found in 2012 in Southern Morocco.

- **Venus**

Venus is the second brightest natural object in the night sky after the Moon.

- **Mars**

Mars might have frozen water, there might have been water on mars even before there were any humans on Earth.

- **Jupiter**

The red dot is a storm with lots of wind. The winds there can reach speeds of 432 km/h, which is faster than any car you can buy.

- **Saturn**

The wind at Saturn's equator can reach speeds as fast as 1,800 km/h. That's almost five times faster than a Bugatti Chiron 300+.

- **Uranus**

These are all Uranus's moons:

1. Titania
2. Umbriel
3. Oberon
4. Ariel
5. Miranda
6. Puck
7. Cressida
8. Desdemona
9. Perdita
10. Setebos
11. Stephano
12. Sycorax
13. Trinculo
14. Ophelia

15. Caliban
16. Cordelia
17. Mab
18. Juliet
19. Belinda
20. Portia
21. Francisco
22. Margaret
23. Cupid
24. Rosalind
25. Bianca
26. Ferdinand
27. Prospero
- **Neptune**

Rocket called 'Voyer 2' is the only rocket to visit Neptune.

Visit this website for a surprise:
https://solarsystem.nasa.gov/solar-system/our-solar-system/overview/

The End